ECCLESIASTES
The Search for Meaning

BY SELWYN HUGHES

QUIET TIME

Jesus, forgive me
for the selfishness of
hurt feelings and
insensitivity
to the needs
of those around me.
Give me your
keen sight and hearing
to know just where to spread
the healing ointment
of your love.
Please provide a supply
just right for today.
And Lord, tie a string
around my heart
reminding me that
this is your day, not mine.

SILENCE!
For Reading and Meditation: Ecclesiastes 1:1–2

" 'Meaningless! Meaningless!' says the Teacher.
'Utterly meaningless! Everything is meaningless.' " (v. 2)

We begin now a study of what has been described as "the most dangerous book in the Bible" – the book of Ecclesiastes. Why dangerous? Because in it one comes face to face with the utter futility of trying to find happiness and meaning in the things of time. And that discovery, for some people could lead to opting out of life altogether.

An old Jewish tradition says that when the sages met to fix the canon of the Old Testament, they debated fiercely whether or not to include a book that was so full of cynicism and doubt. But prayer and wisdom prevailed, and the book was included in the canon. I myself am satisfied that Solomon is the author of Ecclesiastes, although there is much scholarly discussion about this.

The main message of the book comes through in its opening statement: *"Everything is meaningless."* Seeing the utter futility of life is the first step to an encounter with God. Many are not ready to meet with the Lord until they have been silenced by the futility of this world in which they live. I heard someone say that the first book of the Bible everyone ought to read is the book of Ecclesiastes – *because it silences you.* When we see as clearly as Solomon saw that the world does not provide us with the life for which our souls were created, then we are more likely to turn to the true source of happiness – the eternal God Himself.

One of the reasons why some us do not know God well is because we have never been convinced of the utter futility of trying to find life in *things*. We have not been silenced. Let Ecclesiastes silence you, and in that silence you may experience a deeper awareness of God.

The true source of happiness – the eternal God Himself.

O God my Father, if my soul needs silencing, then use Your Word once again to accomplish that task. Do whatever is necessary to bring me to the realisation that what my soul longs for can only be fully found in You. Amen.

LIFE WITHOUT GOD

For Reading and Meditation: Ecclesiastes 1:3–11

"... there is nothing new under the sun." (v.9)

Francis Schaeffer wrote that there are times "when a negative message is needed before anything positive can begin." That sums up the book of Ecclesiastes. In the passage before us today the author begins the task of dragging us through the undeniable facts manifesting the pointlessness and the emptiness of life in order to show us that we must look elsewhere than the world around us for the water that our souls so deeply crave.

Three things are said about life without God – it is boring, fleeting, and repetitive. "What does man gain from all his labour ...?" asks Solomon. Some people enjoy working for a living, but most don't. They watch the clock, fantasise, make up mental games, all designed to fill the time until the work-day is over. If we do not see our work as imitating the creativity of God then it can become exceedingly boring. "Generations come and generations go," says Solomon. We spend just a comparatively short time here on earth and then we are gone. Life is so fleeting. How small and insignificant it makes us feel. Then think about this, continues Solomon. Every morning the sun rises, sets, then the next day the same thing happens ... and the next.

Life on this planet is not all gloom, of course, but who can escape the conclusion that there is something about earth that just does not satisfy? Some graffiti was found on the walls of Bath University: "Do not adjust your life, the fault lies in reality."

Life "under the sun", Solomon has told us, can be boring, fleeting, repetitive, and empty. Life will never be meaningful "under the sun" until we make contact with the One who is above the sun.

"Do not adjust your life, the fault lies in reality."

Gracious and loving Father, wean me off any ideas I may have that life can be found "under the sun". Grant that I might be gripped by the truth that life, real life, is never found in the horizontal but in the Vertical. In You. Amen.

EDUCATION WITHOUT GOD ...
For Reading and Meditation: Ecclesiastes 1:12–18

"For with much wisdom comes much sorrow; the more knowledge, the more grief." (v. 18)

One of the reasons why Solomon uses such forceful language, and so many vivid illustrations, is to break through our defensive attempts to avoid reality. It was T. S. Eliot who said that "humankind cannot bear too much reality". Psychologists warn that we should be careful about stripping away people's defences, as coming face to face with reality too quickly can cause those who are fragile to slide into depression. The author of Ecclesiastes seems unconcerned about this, however, and tells us over and over again, and with deep conviction, that life "under the sun" is futile.

In the passage before us he tells us how his determination to find a purpose for living led him to deep and serious study. But study, and trying to grasp the meaning of the universe by the intellect alone, proved also to be futile. He says that it is like "chasing after the wind" (v. 17). Moffatt translates our text for today: "The more you understand the more you ache."

Life, real life that is, cannot be found through education and intellectual attainment alone. To quote Malcolm Muggeridge: "Education – the great mumbo and fraud of the ages," says this highly educated man, "purports to equip us to live and is prescribed as a universal remedy for everything from juvenile delinquency to premature senility. For the most part it serves to enlarge stupidity, inflate conceit, enhance credulity and puts those subjected to it at the mercy of brainwashing with printing presses, radio and television ..." Lloyd George put it succinctly when he made this caustic comment: "Education without God makes clever devils." Who can deny it?

"Education without God makes clever devils."

O God, save me from the mistake of believing that life is to be found in deep or profound thinking. Help me see that life is to be found in first knowing You, then thinking Your thoughts after You. Teach me to think as You think, dear Lord. In Jesus' Name. Amen.

"SEND IN THE CLOWNS"

For Reading and Meditation: Ecclesiastes 2:1–11

" 'Laughter,' I said, 'is foolish. And what does pleasure accomplish?' " (v. 2)

If education, intellectualism, and philosophy are not the routes to making life work – then what is? Perhaps life can be found in pleasure. Not so, says Solomon. Pleasure pleases, but it is powerless to quench the ache that exists in the soul. We are provided with a list of the ways that pleasure can be gained, but all of them are given the "thumbs down" by Solomon.

The first is laughter. Send in the clowns. Bring on the jokers. Let's hear the funny one-liners. But as almost everyone knows, those who bring laughter to thousands are themselves often desperately unhappy. Billy Graham tells the story of a man who went to a doctor for help with his depression. "I'll give you something better than anti-depressants," said the doctor. "Go and see the clown at the local circus. He has just arrived in the town and is sending people into hysterics." The man looked at the doctor dolefully and said, "I am the clown."

If laughter cannot satisfy then perhaps drink will help. "I tried cheering myself with wine," Solomon tells us ... but clearly that did not satisfy either. He then threw himself into a round of activity – great projects like building a house for himself, planting vineyards, filling his courtyards with slaves, buying up herds and flocks, amassing silver and gold, and finally equipping himself with a harem – what he describes as "the delights of the heart of man" (v. 8). But did these things work? Here's his conclusion: "everything was meaningless, a chasing after the wind" (v. 11). He is not saying, of course, that these things didn't bring pleasure. He is making the point that this kind of pleasure is ephemeral; it just does not last.

Pleasure pleases, but it is powerless to quench the ache that exists in the soul.

My Father and my God, I see I am shut up to You. Earth's fountains are unable to quench the deep thirsts of my soul. To whom shall I go? Only You have the words of eternal life. I am so grateful. Thank You my Father. Amen.

WHERE LIFE ENDS

For Reading and Meditation: Ecclesiastes 2:12–16

*"Like the fool, the wise man too
must die!" (v. 16)*

There are some who believe that the writer of Ecclesiastes had lost all objectivity when he wrote this book, and his pessimistic mood affected everything he looked at. As if anticipating that very argument, he says in verse 9: "In all this my wisdom stayed with me." Disillusioned though he was with the fact that things could not fully satisfy, his objectivity never left him.

In the section before us today he returns to re-examine wisdom, but this time to compare it with folly. We see his mind grappling with the idea: "Shall I be a serious thinker, or just go the way of all fools?" His conclusion, initially anyway, is that wisdom has the advantage over folly: "The wise man has eyes in his head, while the fool walks in the darkness" (v. 14). In other words, it is better to be wise than foolish, better to be learned than ignorant. But would wisdom in itself stop him from slipping towards mean-inglessness? As he ponders that question he comes to the conclusion that if the wise man has eyes to see, what he sees is the limited usefulness of being wise. In one sense it is better to be wise than foolish, but in the final analysis both the wise and the foolish have to face the fact of death. That is a card that "trumps" every other card in life. This, then, is his conclusion: "So what if I do have a fine education? What if I enjoy a good standard of living through the application of common sense? What's the point when it all ends in death?"

The answer, of course, is that there is little or no point if life just ends in death. But the reality is – it doesn't. There is life in the hereafter, and the quality of life in the hereafter depends on what you are after here.

The quality of life in the hereafter depends on what you are after here.

O Father, let me be gripped by the fact, as was the great apostle Paul, that when I know You, life here on earth is too wonderful for words. And to die? That is nothing but gain. All honour and glory be unto Your matchless Name. Amen.

LIFE IN THE REAL WORLD

For Reading and Meditation: Ecclesiastes 2:17–26

"I hated all the things I had toiled for ... because I must leave them to the one who comes after me." (v. 18)

Facing the realities of life can greatly provoke anxiety. The moment when we face the fact that there is nothing in this world – no person, place or thing – that can meet the deepest ache in our soul is probably one of the most solemn moments of our existence. Many can't face that kind of reality so they escape into such things as fantasies, endless rounds of activity, drink, sensual pleasures, and so on. It is this quality – the ability to face reality – that endears Solomon to us. We don't have to guess what is going on inside him. He tells us – and in no uncertain terms.

What is the next thing Solomon turned to in his frustration with life? Work. Solomon is not knocking work, but he is saying that work is not where life is to be found.

It was Oswald Chambers who said: "No Christian makes much progress in the Christian life until he realises that life is more chaotic and tragic than orderly." In other words, life in a fallen world can be tough! The sooner we face that fact and allow it to silence us, the fewer expectations we will have of the world, and the more eagerly we will turn to God.

Up until now God has been left out of Solomon's musings, but as soon as God is brought into the picture, notice the change. Enjoyment, he says, is God's personal gift (v. 25). Satisfaction in things is found only when they are seen as being behind God and not in front of Him. When God is not first, then everything around which we wrap our affections is an idol. There are two paths we can choose: one is to find life in God and enjoy the provision of His hands; the other is to find life in things, and turn our back on God. The latter is "meaningless", says Solomon ... "like chasing after the wind."

Life in a fallen world can be tough!

Father, I see that when You step into my world, then I step out into a new world. Everything looks and appears different. Help me to put nothing in front of You – not even my closest earthly relationship. In Jesus' Name I pray. Amen.

THE TIME TUNNEL

For Reading and Meditation: Ecclesiastes 3:1

"There is a time for everything, and a season for every activity under heaven." (v. 1)

Afer considering the fact that no one is able to make life work apart from God, Solomon turns his attention to the consideration of time. Who can define time? Long-fellow asked, "What is time?", and then went on to say that although time could be measured, it could not be clearly defined.

One of the best definitions of discipleship I think I have ever heard is this: "Discipleship is what a person does with his time." An illustration preachers often use concerning time is this: imagine someone who loves you puts into your personal bank account every day the sum of £1,440 or $1,440, with the stipulation that you have to use it all every day, and anything left over will be cancelled by the bank. Sounds too good to be true, doesn't it? However, Someone who loves you puts into your life every day 1,440 minutes – the gift of time. The same condition applies – you have to use it all, and anything left over is forfeited. So ask yourself now: How do I manage my time? Do I squander it, or see it as a sacred trust?

Solomon's point in drawing our attention to time is to show how life on this earth breaks down into measurable spans. Take a look at how things happen, he seems to be saying, and you will see a controlling schedule behind all things. Does not this in itself suggest that a loving God presides over the circumstances of life? Kierkegaard said: "Life has to be lived forwards but it can only be understood backwards." Pause now for a moment and reflect on how the things you worried about a year ago look so different with hindsight. Aren't you aware that an eternal God has been marshalling your progress in this tunnel of time?

"Disciple-ship is what a person does with his time."

O Father, help me see the issue of time not as a burden, but as a blessing. I want to use my time wisely, but not to become so obsessed by it that I can't stop and smell the roses. Keep me sanely balanced in all this. In Jesus' Name. Amen.

YOU WILL LAUGH AGAIN

For Reading and Meditation: Ecclesiastes 3:2–4

"… a time to weep and a time to laugh, a time to mourn and a time to dance." (v. 4)

Perhaps no better cross-section of life can be found anywhere than in these beautiful and poetic verses. Solomon unfolds for us the variety of life, all of which takes place under the providential hand of God. There are, in fact, fourteen contrasts, and every one of them is familiar to us all.

(1) *There is a time to be born and a time to die.* No one can negotiate his or her arrival into this world, nor the natural time of departure either. Both are beyond our control. (2) *A time to plant and a time to uproot.* Mess around with Mother Nature, for instance, planting when it is time to reap, and you won't get anywhere. Follow the order and you get results; ignore it and you get consequences. (3) *A time to kill and a time to heal.* This is not to be seen as an approval of killing, but a simple statement of fact – wars and killing are part of human life. But so, also, is healing. Charles Swindoll puts it like this: "Life seems strangely fixed between a battlefield and a first aid station, between murder and medicine." It most certainly is.

(4) *A time to tear down and a time to build.* Demolition is followed by construction, then after a while more demolition and more construction. Isn't this a pattern with which every generation is familiar? (5) *A time to weep and a time to laugh.* Both sorrow and laughter are inevitable in every life. Some have more sorrow than laughter, but no one goes through the world without touching both. Are you shedding a lot of tears over some great difficulty or problem at the moment? I promise you in God's Name, sometime, not too far distant in the future, your heart *will* laugh again.

"Life seems strangely fixed between a battlefield and a first aid station, between murder and medicine."

Help me see, dear Father, that though I pass through times of sorrow and difficulty, nothing can shake the rock of existence on which I stand. In sorrow or in laughter may I never lose sight of You. In Jesus' Name I ask it. Amen.

THE END OF SEARCHING
For Reading and Meditation: Ecclesiastes 3:4b–6a

"... a time to scatter stones and a time to gather them ..." (v. 5)

We continue looking at Solomon's fourteen contrasts of life. (6) *A time to mourn and a time to dance.* We lose a loved one, and then, a year or so later, a family member gets married. Mourning is turned to dancing. Isn't this true of almost every family on the earth?

(7) *A time to scatter stones and a time to gather them.* Some commentators believe this refers to scattering stones over a difficult neighbour's field in order to hinder him from ploughing; to then go out and retrieve those stones implies an act of sorrow and repentance. The thought here is that life is punctuated with periods when people seem to go out of their way to make it difficult for others, then they have second thoughts, and do everything they can to cancel out their provocative behaviour. I doubt whether anyone reading these lines has not experienced the truth of these words. (8) *A time to embrace and a time to refrain.* There are times when every one of us needs the quiet embrace of a friend who gets as close to us as possible, and whispers in our ear words of comfort and consolation. But there are times, too, when what we need is not so much consolation but confrontation. We need to be faced with some hard truths. For life to be balanced, both must be part of our experience.

(9) *A time to search and a time to give up.* How much easier life would be for some if they would learn this lesson and give up searching for something they inwardly sense will never be found. It's good to have hope, but hope must be based on something that is realistic. As someone once put it, "It's better to be a sane pessimist than a silly optimist." I agree.

"It's better to be a sane pessimist than a silly optimist."

O Father, how can I sufficiently thank You for helping me to give up searching for satisfaction down paths that were all dead-ends. I need no longer search, for I have found. All honour and glory be to Your peerless and precious Name. Amen.

ONE FOOT IN ETERNITY

For Reading and Meditation: Ecclesiastes 3:6b–8

*"… a time to be silent and a time
to speak …" (v. 7)*

We look now at the last on the list of Solomon's fourteen contrasts. (10) *A time to keep and a time to throw (or give) away.* Think at this moment of all the stuff you might have crammed in your loft or cellar that you will never use. Isn't it better to give it to someone who could make good use of it? Some things you will need to keep, of course, but some things ought to be given away. Perhaps today is the time for doing just that.

(11) *A time to tear and a time to mend.* The idea of not getting anything new but instead patching up everything may at times be right, but at other times it can be wrong. Some things must never be given up – truth, for example. However, we ought not to be afraid of trying out new ways of doing things. It's not a mark of spiritually to be a "stick in the mud". (12) *A time to be silent and a time to speak.* It's not often you hear someone confess, "I feel sorry for the things I did not say," but you will hear many admit: "I wish I knew how to keep my mouth shut." The sooner we learn when to talk and when to listen the better it will be for us – and for others!

(13) *A time to love and a time to hate.* Love that does not have another person's interests at heart is not love, but mere sentimentality. To love means you must also be willing to hate. Not people, but the thing that may be hindering them from fulfilling their spiritual potential. (14) *A time for war and a time for peace.* Wars start, it is said, "when someone has something somebody else wants." As I write, there are over sixty wars going on somewhere in the world. Solomon's words, therefore, rise to almost cosmic proportions: "there must be a time also for peace."

The sooner we learn when to talk and when to listen the better!

My Father and my God, this focus on the events that take place in time drives home to me my need to have one foot also in eternity. I am grateful that although a creature of time, because I am in You I am bound for eternity. Amen.

ALL THINGS BEAUTIFUL

For Reading and Meditation: Ecclesiastes 3:9–11

*"He has made everything beautiful
in its time." (v. 11)*

Solomon returns to familiar territory in the verses before us today, and follows up his poetic appraisal of time with a question: "What benefit do we get from time?" It might seem a blessing, but actually it is a burden. As he looks at the interesting cycles of time he concludes that without God all is boring and futile. But here's a sentence that brushes aside futility: *"He has made everything beautiful in its time."* To look at time through mere human eyes alone is to see it as interesting but futile; to look at it through the lens of faith is to see a beautiful picture coming together under the hands of the Divine Artist. He takes our sorrows and turns them into symphonies; He takes our tears and turns them into telescopes; He takes our calamities and turns them into opportunities.

If you could see through your troubles at this moment and catch sight of the beautiful picture God is painting as He mixes the blacks and blues, the reds and crimsons with the whites of His purposes, you would never again shake your fist in His face and tell Him that your life is a mess. The timing of things may not be as you would like them to be but remember, He is making everything beautiful – *in its time.*

God has set eternity in our hearts, yet we cannot understand what He has done. At first it doesn't seem to make much sense. God has not only established a timetable by which everything is ordered, but He has also placed within our spirits a deep longing for eternity. This nostalgia we have for heaven is built into every human being, and although with many it is denied, ignored, or overlaid with other things, indisputably it is there.

The Divine Artist takes our sorrows and turns them into symphonies.

O God, it seems too good to be true – that the thing most of humanity is searching for, I have found. You are the Homeland of my soul. In You I am safe, steady, and growing. I shall be eternally grateful. Amen.

GOD-GIVEN ABILITIES

For Reading and Meditation: Ecclesiastes 3:12–15

"That everyone may eat and drink, and find satisfaction in all his toil – this is the gift of God." (v. 13)

Solomon's main point gets clearer every moment – without God in our lives, life can be pretty boring and empty. But when God is in our lives, His presence makes a world of difference. Look with me now at four things God gives us so that we might enjoy our life here.

First, *He gives us the ability to be happy* (v. 12). Happiness is not something we earn; it is a gift. Only God can give us the perspective on life that enables us to remain happy even when things don't go our way. Second, *God gives us the ability to do good* (v. 12). Any one of us can be good to those who are good to us, but it takes God to help us be good to those who are not good to us. That ability flows from God's heart of love and compassion into ours.

Third, *God gives us the ability to eat and drink* (v. 13). Have you ever considered that your appetite is something that comes from God? Fourth, *God gives us the ability to see good in our labour* (v. 13). The whole workplace could be transformed overnight if men and women saw it from God's perspective. Instead of asking, "What is the least I can do for a day's wages?", our question would be: "What is the most I can do for a day's wages?" Hard to take? That's because it is an "above the sun" perspective.

"God is ever bringing back what disappears."

However ragged life may seem in a fallen world, the Creator knows no such imperfections. Everything He does, we are told, remains for ever. The Almighty builds things to last. And what He does is not only permanent, but complete: "nothing can be added to it, nothing can be taken from it" (v. 14). Moffatt translates verse 15: "God is ever bringing back what disappears." God repeats situations in our lives until we learn the lessons they are meant to teach us. God wants to make a permanent lesson out of something we think is merely passing and temporary.

O God, I go through the same situations time and again simply because I have not heeded Your voice. Make me alert to each passing moment, and show me how to draw from it the lessons You want to teach me. In Jesus' Name. Amen.

THE PATIENCE OF GOD

For Reading and Meditation: Ecclesiastes 3:16–17

" 'God will bring to judgment both the righteous
and the wicked ...' " (v. 17)

Ever found yourself feeling frustrated because of the way in which wickedness seems to win over justice? Then you know something of how Solomon feels in the verses before us today. Every generation, throughout time, has had to face this problem. James Russell Lowell put it this way:

> *Truth forever on the scaffold,*
> *Wrong forever on the throne.*

Solomon struggles, as no doubt you have done (and perhaps still do), with the fact that in the very place where you would expect to see justice, you find wickedness and corruption prevailing. In the days when I was a pastor, I often went to court with people who had a genuine case to be heard, only to see it broken down by tactics that were dishonest or unjust. This was not always so, of course, and is more the exception than the rule, but I have seen enough injustice in my time to share something of Solomon's cynicism.

Am I talking today, I wonder, to someone who is at this moment a victim of judicial injustice? Then don't allow yourself to become too cynical, for, as Solomon said: "God will bring to judgment both the righteous and the wicked ..." Wrong will not continue for ever. The day is coming when all corruption and injustice will be called to judgment before the throne of God's truth. But of course, being human, we wish the injustices we have received could be put right – now. God seems to be much more patient than we are, and what we must do is to ask for grace to be patient with the patience of God.

We must ask for grace to be patient with the patience of God.

O God my Father, give me the divine perspective on things so that present injustices may be swallowed up in the long-term purposes. Help me see that I will have my day in court – Your court. In Jesus' Name I ask it. Amen.

HOW ERROR OCCURS

For Reading and Meditation: Ecclesiastes 3:18–22

" 'Man's fate is like that of the animals ...
As one dies, so dies the other.' " (v. 19)

Have you noticed that whenever Solomon looks "above the sun" he gets the right perspective, but when he looks "beneath the sun" his blood pressure rises, along with his cynicism? We said yesterday that when he looked away from the injustice he observed on earth to the day when all wrongs would be righted, he appeared to be in a better frame of mind, but in the verses before us today he has descended into deep cynicism again. This is what happens when we don't keep our eyes on God – we come to the same exasperating and heretical conclusions as Solomon.

Listen to what he says: we are like the animals, and will end up like animals – in oblivion. Solomon's cynicism drives him to make a statement that might seem justified under the circumstances, but is quite untrue. We are different from animals and bound for a different destiny. Solomon is not talking truth here; he is talking cynicism. This is what happens when we take our eyes off God, and the truths He unfolds in His Word – we can descend into making the same kind of rash and heretical statements as Solomon. His words are the musings of a confused cynic and represent what he felt at the time, but they are not to be taken as true for they are contradicted in other parts of Scripture.

Cynicism confuses; Scripture clarifies.

We ought never to forget as Christians that unless we have a full Biblical perspective on issues we too can descend into making rash and heretical statements just as Solomon did. Cynicism numbs us spiritually and leaves us feeling downcast and disillusioned. A full view of Scripture, however, lifts us up and gives us God's perspectives. Cynicism confuses; Scripture clarifies.

O Father, how thankful I am that You have given me a Book which enables me to have the right perspective on all things. Teach me how to compare one scripture with another. To say not merely "it is written", but "it is written again". In Jesus' Name. Amen.

IT'S LONELY AT THE TOP

For Reading and Meditation: Ecclesiastes 4:1–12

"Better one handful with tranquillity than two handfuls with toil and chasing after the wind." (v. 6)

Solomon "looks around", as he puts it, sees people caught in the grip of oppression, and his heart is filled with despair. His cynicism reaches new depths when he concludes that those who had died were fortunate, and the unborn were in an even better position. Some commentators see these sentiments as marking the lowest point in the book. The competitiveness that he sees causes him to say once again that life is meaningless. It's not healthy competition he is referring to here, but the savage, ruthless, brutal, dog-eat-dog mentality that rides roughshod over people's feelings. Moffatt puts the answer beautifully when he translates verse 6 thus: "Still, one handful of content is better than two hands full of toil and futile effort." It is.

But money and possessions are not much good when you have no one to share them with. Life lived on this level, says Solomon, is also meaningless.

He then makes a statement which is often misunderstood: "Two are better than one ... If one falls down, his friend can help him up ... if two lie down together, they will keep warm" (vv. 9–11). Note the emphasis in these sayings is on two people. But at the end of the passage Solomon says something very strange: "A cord of three strands is not quickly broken." The point being made here is this – when you are in a close relationship with someone you love and who loves you, you not only have what the other person gives you, but you have a third quality – a strength and power which unfolds from out of the relationship, and which you could never have experienced if you had stayed apart. There is no comfort quite like a friend when you are forced to live on "the ragged edge of time".

There is no comfort quite like a friend when you are forced to live on "the ragged edge of time".

Father, I see that I am built for relationships, not only with You, but with others also. And in a relationship lies a power that is greater than the sum of its two parts. May I discover more of this. In Christ's Name I ask it. Amen.

THE BEST FRIEND

For Reading and Meditation: Ecclesiastes 4:13–16

"Better a poor but wise youth than an old but foolish king who no longer knows how to take warning." (v. 13)

We ended yesterday by saying that there is no comfort quite like a friend when you are forced to live on "the ragged edge of time". Yet strange though it may sound, it is possible to have many friends and still be lonely. That's the point Solomon is making in the verses that are before us today.

Look again at the picture he presents to us in verse 13. It is a picture of two people: one a poor but wise youth, the other an old but rich king. Who would you think has the advantage? The king? Not so, says Solomon. He may have more experience of life, but something more than experience is needed if we are to walk effectively through the world. What we need is – wisdom. Experience without wisdom is of little benefit. It's not how many hours we have lived that counts, but what we have gained from those hours that is important.

The whole of chapter 4 has been taken up with the issue of loneliness, and Solomon ends by underlining the fact that it is not our circumstances that makes us lonely, but our inability to apply wisdom to our situation. Take two people who are in exactly the same circumstances. Both are surrounded by agreeable and helpful companions. One enjoys the company of friends, but the other complains that he is lonely. Where lies the problem with the one who feels lonely? Not in the circumstances, but in the "innerstances" – his attitudes. He lacks the wisdom to see that no human being can provide him with the comfort which the soul so deeply craves. That is found only in God. The wise are those who understand that while human friends are important, the best friend to have is God.

Experience without wisdom is of little benefit.

My Father and my God, grant me the wisdom to understand that whilst the making and keeping of earthly friendships is important, the making and keeping of Your friendship is even more important. In Jesus' Name. Amen.

WATCH YOUR STEP

For Reading and Meditation: Ecclesiastes 5:1–3

*"Guard your steps when you go to
the house of God." (v. 1)*

I n this chapter we catch Solomon in one of those rare moments when he breaks free of his cynical frame of mind – so let's make the most of it! God's people, Solomon is saying, are far too casual in their approach to worship. Familiarity may not breed contempt, but it certainly can breed insensitivity.

The way we approach God's house will determine what we receive at God's house. When we make our way to God's house we ought to be spiritually alert, intent on hearing what God has to say to us, and spiritually expectant. "Bad preaching," said one famous Bible expositor, "is God's curse on an unexpectant congregation." If you are not hearing God when you go to church the problem is not that God is not speaking; it is more likely that you have stopped listening.

Solomon's advice on the subject of vows is quite simple: First, don't delay in delivering it (v. 5), and second, don't deny you said it (v. 6). Have you made a vow to God and never followed through on it? Ask God's forgiveness and the grace, if the vow is still capable of being undertaken, to do what you promised. We live in an age when vows and commitments do not seem as important as once they did. God keeps His vows; so should we. Let's heed this important message of Solomon; babbling, rambling, and ill-considered words, though found in many places, ought not to be found in church. It's no good opening your mouth wide and having a good sing if you only open half an ear and never get around to doing what you promised to God.

> *The way we approach God's house will determine what we receive at God's house.*

O God, help me see what tension I set up inside myself when I make vows to You that I do not keep. You keep Your word to me, may I also keep my word to You. Help me, where it is possible, to catch up on any unfulfilled promises. In Christ's Name I pray. Amen.

MONEY! MONEY! MONEY!

For Reading and Meditation: Ecclesiastes 5:8–12

"Whoever loves money never has money enough ..." (v. 10)

Solomon is now being cynical again. The rich tend to be the leaders, he says, and the poor the followers. Those with wealth are usually the most influential, and they are expert at appointing officials to watch over officials. In time, the "red tape" becomes so thick that the poor have no hope of cutting through it. Solomon is not the only one who is cynical about bureaucracy; I have to admit, sometimes I feel the same way too. His main point, however, is to show us that wealth is not everything. As Derek Tidball puts it: "Money ... increases your appetite but not your satisfaction."

There is nothing wrong with possessing money, of course; it is when money is allowed to possess you that trouble comes. To be money-mad is to be a candidate for misery. My father wrote on the flyleaf of my Bible the day after I was converted: "Money is a universal provider for everything but happiness and a passport everywhere but to heaven." Wise words which I have never forgotten. Wealthy people, says Solomon, find it difficult to sleep because they are worried about their investments. The more money you have, the more you have to worry over. Someone put it like this: "More money, more worry, more worry, less sleep."

All this, of course, refers to those who have no sense of stewardship, for when money is surrendered to God, then money becomes a "trust" – a "trust" which is owned by God. We are not meant to be proprietors, but trustees of the Lord's money. God is the owner of everything on the face of the earth, and we are the owers. All giving ought to be out of gratitude for what He has given to us.

"Money ... increases your appetite but not your satisfaction."

Father, help me in relation to material things to see that I am a steward, not a proprietor; a servant, not a master; an ower, not an owner. Change my perspectives so that I look at everything from Your point of view. In Christ's Name I pray. Amen.

GOLD – OR GOD?

For Reading and Meditation: Ecclesiastes 5:13–20

"Naked a man comes from his mother's womb, and
as he comes, so he departs." (v. 15)

Solomon is still harping on about money. Pretty boring you might think. But isn't he putting his finger on the pulse of our problems? We try to find in gold what we ought to be finding in God.

Solomon forces us to consider how foolish it is to try and find security in something that is so uncertain. Consider this, says Solomon: "Savings are put into risky investments that turn sour, and soon there is nothing left to pass on to one's son. The man who speculates is soon back to where he began – with nothing ... all his hard work has been for nothing; he has been working for the wind. It is all swept away. All the rest of his life he is under a cloud – gloomy, discouraged, frustrated, and angry" (vv. 14–17, TLB). Clearly, the soul's security cannot be found in money. When will men and women learn this?

No doubt you are aware by now that Solomon does not allow us to stay too long in the darkness of his cynicism without seeking to throw some light across the road. First, he says, set your face against the idea that happiness lies in possessing material things, and refuse to put a priority on making money just for the sake of it. Take life as it comes, laugh a little bit more, and try to find pleasure in the simple things. Second, enjoy your work. It will not meet the deep needs of your soul, but it is good to be engaged in a task, however menial it may be. Third, see everything God has given you as a gift rather than something you have earned. A grateful spirit ought not to be far from any of us.

How blessed are those who find that God keeps their hearts "occupied with gladness". All the riches in the world, all the honours, all the accolades, all the applause, all the achievements, are as nothing compared to the joy of having one's heart occupied by the King of kings.

A grateful spirit ought not to be far from any of us.

O God my Father, help me put a sign on my heart that says: "Occupied by the King of kings." Then, when lesser things seek to invade my soul, they will see that there is no more room, and leave to go on their way. Amen.

SOURCE OF CONTENTMENT

For Reading and Meditation: Ecclesiastes 6:1–6

*"God gives a man wealth, possessions and honour …
but God does not enable him to enjoy them …" (v. 2)*

In this chapter Solomon continues to focus on those whom we generally refer to as "well heeled". But he draws our attention to an issue which he has not covered before, namely the plight of those who have everything life can offer yet are prevented from enjoying it, not by circumstances, but by God Himself.

At first it seems almost unbelievable that God would allow someone to have the good things of life, then dampen the feelings of pleasure that these things can bring. Why would God do this? When God acts to deny people enjoyment it is because He wants to show them that He is the One who enables men and women to experience pleasure in things; the things themselves do not give pleasure.

That might sound manipulative to some, but divine love never exploits. Those who make money their god will never find contentment. Any god that usurps the place of the true God puts the soul "out of joint", so to speak. The power to give contentment belongs to God alone.

There is nothing wrong in enjoying one's family (indeed Scripture encourages it). However, even the most loving family is powerless to quench the ache that resides deep in the human psyche. Money can keep a big family going, but it can't meet the needs of the heart. As Solomon reflects on this he becomes cynical again, and says that it is better to be a stillborn child than to be caught up in the meaningless nonsense of trying to find life outside of God.

In my experience, those who are honest enough to admit to deep inner emptiness yearn for a shorter life rather than a longer one. In the end, to those who do not know God, it makes no difference whether they have been rich or poor.

The power to give contentment belongs to God alone.

O God, I see now why this book is designed to silence me. For nothing can satisfy my soul except You. I need to take this lesson on board, for I tend to rely more on the visible than the Invisible. Help me, dear Father. In Jesus' Name. Amen.

WHERE IS YOUR IDENTITY?

For Reading and Meditation: Ecclesiastes 6:7–9

"All man's efforts are for his mouth, yet his appetite is never satisfied." (v. 7)

I
f having a large family or living a thousand years does not meet the needs of the soul – then what does? Hard work perhaps? No, says cynical Solomon, not even that. Moffatt translates our text for today thus: "A man toils on to satisfy his hunger, but his wants are never met."

Nothing brings satisfaction to a life where God is absent, not even hard work. Psychologists talk nowadays about A-type personalities, people who are obsessed with work. These people, it has been discovered, see their whole identity in terms of what they do rather than who they are. God help us if we see our identity in terms of our accomplishments rather than in being the objects of divine love. What will happen to us when we can't work any more, can't accomplish? It's interesting that the word "appetite" in our reading today is the Hebrew word *nephesh*, or "soul". What it is saying to us is this – the soul can never be satisfied with anything less than God. And, Solomon adds, not even a bright mind, and a good education, can do so either. Both the fools and the wise end up in the same place if they do not know God.

If you could put a stethoscope on the soul you would hear a rumbling which, if translated into words, would sound something like this: "I'm so hungry ... so thirsty ... why won't someone give me what I really long for?" And what does the soul long for? God. Far too many Christians try to make their souls work with things rather than God. When we get more satisfaction out of the things we do for God, rather than from God Himself, then we are in serious spiritual danger. Nothing fully satisfies the soul. Nothing, that is, apart from God.

The soul can never be satisfied with anything less than God.

O God my Father, forgive me if I seek my identity in the things I do rather than finding it in who I am. Show me even more clearly than ever that Your estimation of me is not based on my performance but on the fact that I belong to You. Amen.

STOP ARGUING!

For Reading and Meditation: Ecclesiastes 6:10–12

"… no man can contend with one who is stronger than he." (v. 10)

Solomon is "above the sun" now, putting the focus once again on God. "At life's core," says Dr Larry Crabb, "the real issues are theological issues." What he means is that when life is brought down to its irreducible minimum, the issue always is – God. What do we make of *Him*? How does He fit into our lives? Is He in charge, or is He not?

Have you not found that whenever you make sure God is in His place, everything around you falls into place too? You see things from a different perspective. God is sovereign, Solomon is saying here, and the sooner we recognise that the better. A purpose was written into the universe long before we arrived, and though at times it may look as if God is not in control, this is not so. And, he adds, because God is bigger than we are, it is useless to put ourselves in conflict with Him (v. 10). C. S. Lewis put it well when he said in *The Problem of Pain*: "To argue with God is to argue with the very power that makes it possible to argue at all."

Solomon's last point in this chapter is to bring us face to face with the fact that we do not know the future, and his message, by implication, is that if we are wise we will get to know the One who knows the future. Knowing God means we come in touch with the only One who can really meet our soul's deepest needs. Contentment does not lie in a large bank balance, status, ambition, material possessions, or earthly success. It comes only when we are in a close relationship with God. Only He can give us the power to enjoy life. We would be wise to build on God, not on gold.

"To argue with God is to argue with the very power that makes it possible to argue at all."

O God, help me this day to stand before You with an open heart, an open mind, and an open being. For I want to be changed not into the image of things, but into the image of You. I will have no idols in my life. I own You as my only Lord. Amen.

"BETTER THAN CHANEL NO 5"

For Reading and Meditation: Ecclesiastes 7:1

*"A good name is better than
fine perfume ..." (v. 1)*

We are now at the half-way mark of the book of Ecclesiastes, and one notices immediately a change of perspective. Solomon's cynicism does not altogether disappear, but a new note is being struck which rings out most clearly in this chapter and then continues to the end of the book. That new note is – wisdom. As wisdom begins to break through into Solomon's perspective, he changes from a narrative style to a proverbial style, and its effect is as dramatic as the sun breaking through the clouds on a dark and stormy day. He begins this chapter with a series of seven comparative proverbs, all built around the word "better". Let's focus on them one by one.

First, "A good name is *better* than fine perfume." A modern translation of that might read: "A good name is better than Chanel No 5." When we say a person has a good name we mean, of course, that he or she has a good character. And nothing is more important than character. It has been said that reputation is what others think of us, character is what we are deep down inside. Take care of your character and your reputation will take care of itself.

Second, "the day of death [is] *better* than the day of birth" (v. 1). Is this really so? If it is then ought we to be mourning people's birth and celebrating at their death? Solomon seems to be turning life on its head. Why? Because the days that follow our death (for those whose hearts are right with God, that is) are more joyous and carefree than those that follow our birth. It's good to feel "at home" with those who love us in this life, but much better, as the old hymn puts it, to be "at home with the Lord".

Take care of your character and your reputation will take care of itself.

O God, You are the centre of all my values, the centre of my life. Can this life die within me? It cannot die any more than You can die. Death is the end of one life and beginning of a new one. I rest in glad assurance. Thank You my Father. Amen.

WISE ADVICE!

For Reading and Meditation: Ecclesiastes 7:2–10

*"Do not be quickly provoked in your spirit,
for anger resides in the lap of fools." (v. 9)*

We continue looking at the rest of Solomon's comparative proverbs. Third, "It is *better* to go to a house of mourning than to go to a house of feasting" (v. 2). Again, this doesn't seem to make much sense to the natural mind, but remember, wisdom always sees beneath the surface of things. What Solomon is meaning is this – you are more likely to come face to face with reality in a funeral parlour than a restaurant. And being unwilling to face reality is to be ill-prepared for dealing with life.

Fourth, "Sorrow is *better* than laughter" (v. 3). Really? Yes really. After a quick laugh, it's amazing how what we laughed about is so easily forgotten. It's not the same, however, with sorrow. Any preacher will tell you the best audience to address is a funeral audience. They listen with rapt attention. Fifth, "It is *better* to heed a wise man's rebuke than to listen to the song of fools" (v. 5). We much prefer to listen to a song that's making its way up the charts than to listen to a rebuke, but in the long run the rebuke will do us the more good. I thank God for the rebukes I have had in my time. They have helped shape me and my character.

Sixth, "The end of a matter is *better* than its beginning" (v. 8). The way things end is reality. The whole picture is on display. Fantasies are over, truth is all that can be seen. We ought to learn from that and be more realistic in our projections and aims. Seventh, "Patience is *better* than pride" (v. 8). Are you one of those who prays: "Lord give me patience ... and give it to me right now!"? Beneath a patient spirit is a groundswell of wisdom. Pride pushes wisdom aside, and when that happens, then it is easy to play the role of a fool.

> *Being unwilling to face reality is to be ill-prepared for dealing with life.*

My Father and my God, I have gathered some wisdom on my journey through life, but now I pray for the kind of wisdom that is greater and sharper than all earthly wisdom – Your wisdom. Make me a wise person, my Father. In Jesus' Name. Amen.

For Reading and Meditation: Ecclesiastes 7:11–14

"... the advantage of knowledge is this:
that wisdom preserves the life of its possessor." (v. 12)

Having previously focused our attention on the dangers and disadvantages of folly, Solomon now invites us to look at the benefits and advantages of wisdom.

"Wisdom is a shelter," he says (v. 12). It protects us from pitfalls or from entering into foolish schemes and ideas. Wisdom protects us from being overtaken by an unexpected financial crisis, for example, by showing us the importance of "saving for a rainy day". Wisdom tells us that we should make sure our liabilities never exceed our assets, that it is better, whenever possible, to avoid temptation than to confront it, that to harbour resentment is like harbouring a snake in your bosom, and so on. If you possess wisdom than you won't fall apart under pressure. Wisdom won't stop you experiencing problems, but it will protect you from unnecessary ones.

The second thing Solomon says about wisdom is that it gives us a clearer perspective on life. He asks: "Who can straighten what he has make crooked?" (v. 13). How we wish we could, but sometimes such a thing is beyond us. Wisdom will help us to focus only on the things that can be changed, and not to spend useless time and energy in trying to change the unchangeable. A divine thread of sovereignty runs through our lives, points out Solomon, so whether times are good or bad – be happy. Wisdom enables us to see that everything is under God's control – the up times and the down times, the "in" times and the "out" times. We are not the victims of blind fate or random chance. God is over all things and in control of all things. Thus we are people of destiny.

Wisdom won't stop you experiencing problems, but it will protect you from unnecessary ones.

O Father, help me trace Your hand in the whole of my life, not just the "good" bits. May I see that the setbacks as well as the successes are part of Your purpose for me, and thus praise You in everything. "Through good or ill You are with me still." Thank You, dear Father. Amen.

KEEP YOUR BALANCE!

For Reading and Meditation: Ecclesiastes 7:15–18

"The man who fears God will avoid all [extremes]." (v. 18)

One perplexing situation for which wisdom and a divine perspective is needed, says Solomon, is when we see the righteous suffer and the wicked prosper. This is an issue with which young Christians often struggle, but it is a problem that is as old as life itself. The psalmist struggled with it (particularly in Psalm 73), and so have millions since.

Idi Amin, the tyrant who once ruled Uganda, lives on, while a missionary family on their way to bring help and medical care to others are lost in a plane crash. You can't make sense of that unless you have an unshakeable trust in God, and believe that one day (not now) He will answer every question to our satisfaction.

The second issue for which wisdom and a divine perspective is needed is the matter of spiritual balance. "Do not be over-righteous" is his advice (v. 16). He is thinking here, I believe, of those who (forgive the cliché) are too heavenly minded to be of any earthly good. I know people who think they are head over heels in love with the Lord, but who have no love for others. The apostle John calls these people "liars" (1 John 4:20). Super-spirituality is out, says Solomon; it's an extreme. But lest we go to the other extreme he speaks out against this also: "Do not be over-wicked" (v. 17). What this means is that all of us, because of the Fall, have a wicked streak within us, and we should watch that we do not indulge that. He is not saying you can get away with a little wickedness. Far from it. He is saying don't give way to it. Solomon is pleading for moderation, and only as you see this can you understand what he is saying. Extremes and excesses are destructive. Keep your balance.

Extremes and excesses are destructive. Keep your balance.

O God, teach me how to avoid all excesses and extremes so that I might be a truly balanced Christian. I would shun over-spirituality as I would shun unbridled urges and lusts. Help me, my Father. In Jesus' Name. Amen.

WISDOM – ONLY FROM GOD

For Reading and Meditation: Ecclesiastes 7:19–24

"Whatever wisdom may be, it is far off and most profound – who can discover it?" (v. 24)

Wisdom provides us with an inner strength. That is the point Solomon is making in this passage. One who operates with wisdom possesses more strength than ten city officials. And those who have come up against officialdom and bureaucracy will know that that is some strength! When we have wisdom, we have the inner strength to cope with whatever comes – tensions, stresses and problems that are not easily resolved.

Solomon goes on to point out, however, that the possession of wisdom does not mean we become popular. You will still get criticised, he tells us, but don't let that throw you. "You may hear your servant cursing you ... many times you yourself have cursed others" (vv. 21–22). A friend once shared with me his formula for handling criticism. "When people criticise me," he said, "I am thankful they don't know how bad I really am, or they would have much worse to say." I have found that very helpful and I hope you do too. As Chuck Swindoll puts it: "Give God thanks that people are just hitting the visible, not the whole truth."

Solomon's next statement about wisdom is one we must not overlook: "'I [was] determined to be wise' – but this was beyond me" (v. 23). Solomon found in seeking wisdom that wisdom was not easy to find. Why is that? Because whilst we have an innate ability to gather knowledge, we cannot be wise without the help of God. Solomon did not make this next statement, but nevertheless, this is what he is saying: "If any of you lacks wisdom, he should ask God, who gives generously to all without finding fault" (James 1:5). You can find knowledge in the world, but wisdom – true wisdom, that is – comes only from God.

When we have wisdom, we have the inner strength to cope with whatever comes.

O God, I bow before You and acknowledge that the wisdom I need to handle life I just haven't got. I fail to see the things I ought to see and value the things I ought to value. Give me Your wisdom, dear Father – heavenly wisdom. In Jesus' Name I ask it. Amen.

WHAT'S SCARCE?

For Reading and Meditation: Ecclesiastes 7:25–29

"... I found one [upright] man among a thousand ..." (v. 28)

Wisdom was something very important to Solomon. You may remember it was this that he prayed for when God said to him: "Ask for whatever you want me to give you" (1 Kings 3:5–9). Notwithstanding God's promise to grant his request, Solomon had set out to discover all he could about earthly wisdom. He talked to knowledgeable people, dialogued with scholars and scribes, but when he put all his findings together he concluded human wisdom was not all it was cracked up to be.

His next remark, one that some would say is extremely sexist, makes the point that whilst wisdom was elusive, so also was righteousness, and although he had found one righteous man in a thousand, he had not found one righteous woman at all. Does this mean that men are better than women? Of course not. Solomon is just making a comparison which in his culture would not have the connotation it has today. He is using what we call hyperbole – an exaggerated statement made for emphasis. Even if he was saying that men are better than women then, as R. Gordis points out: "When you work out his figures men are only one tenth of one per cent better than women."

The real point he is making is seen in the last verse of the chapter – righteousness is scarce. And why? Well, it's not God's fault, because in the beginning He made humankind pure and upright. But tragedy struck, and through the wilful disobedience of Adam and Eve, sin invaded our human nature. Clearly, then, our problems are not God's fault, but ours. They are not around us, but within us. We can't blame anyone other than ourselves for our lack of righteousness. The reason why we are not righteous is because we don't want to be.

Right-eousness is scarce.

Father, I am so thankful that although I cannot find righteousness in myself, I can find it in You. Through Christ's sacrifice for me on Calvary I have righteousness not merely imputed to me, but imparted to me. I am eternally grateful. Amen.

A SELF-PORTRAIT

For Reading and Meditation: Ecclesiastes 8:1

"Who knows the explanation of things?
Wisdom brightens a man's face ..." (v. 1)

There is a centuries-old saying that goes like this: "Wise men are rarely academics, and academics are rarely wise men." Whether or not that is true I do not know, but what I do know from reading Solomon's writings is this – *wisdom* is not something academic; it is designed to have a practical outworking in our lives. Many commentators believe that Solomon is giving us a self-portrait here, and is using himself as an illustration of how wisdom works in the lives of those who have a position of authority over others. Look at the text before us again. Two things are said about a wise man in authority: first, he has an understanding of the big picture, and second, he has a cheerful disposition.

Take the first – *seeing the big picture*. Those who are not leaders concentrate on how to bring their skills to bear on the task in front of them – the "how"; those who are leaders, however, concentrate on the wider perspective – the "why". That is the reason why, as someone put it: "the person who knows *how* will usually have a job but that person will usually work for the one who knows *why*." The follower needs to know how, the leader needs to know why.

The second qualification of those who are called to lead is this – *a cheerful disposition*. Nothing is more contagious than cheerfulness. Leaders are more often than not scared people – scared they might not lead well. Thus their faces become stern, hard, unsmiling, and intense. Wisdom, the kind that comes from God that is, lights up the face. Thus the face more often than not radiates cheerfulness. A face that is always stern is not a face that reflects wisdom.

Nothing is more contagious than cheerfulness.

Father, whether I am a leader or not, give me a face that reflects Your wisdom. I know I am not responsible for the face I started life with, but I am responsible for the face I finish up with. May my face reflect Your face. In Jesus' Name. Amen.

MORE LEADERSHIP QUALITIES

For Reading and Meditation: Ecclesiastes 8:2–8

"As no-one is discharged in time of war, so wickedness will not release those who practise it." (v. 8)

Whoever you are, and whatever position of authority you hold in life, you will be well advised to heed Solomon's thoughts on the qualities of a wise leader. We have already examined two, now we look at another three.

The third quality is this – *a high regard for authority*. "Obey the king's command," (v. 2) says Solomon, or in other words, respect whoever is over you in authority. Those who have no respect for those higher than them will never get the respect of those under them. For those under them will sense they are not loyal to the ones above them, and the whole chain of command will be negatively affected. This is a major problem in industry and business today – a problem that could be solved by following Solomon's wise advice.

A fourth quality is this – *be willing to ride out the tough times without withdrawing your support* (vv. 3–4). If there are clearly sinful practices going on, that is another issue. But that apart, Solomon is telling us that you can't change authority unless you are higher than it, so the thing to do is to work effectively from beneath. Not by subversive or rebellious attempts, but by applying the fifth quality of leadership – *knowing when and how to appeal* (vv. 5–6). Timing is crucial. Many have ruined situations because they did the right thing at the wrong time. "The wise heart will know the proper time and procedure" (v. 5).

The final words of this passage (vv. 7–8) remind us that everyone has their limitations, even those in the highest echelons of authority. There's a final bottom line from which all leaders must operate. It is the fact that all of us, bosses included, must one day die.

Many have ruined situations because they did the right thing at the wrong time.

O Father, I see that no matter what position of power I have in life, I can do nothing to redirect the wind or change the fact that one day I will die. May this understanding evoke in me a continuous attitude of deep humility. In Jesus' Name. Amen.

HOW TO HANDLE MYSTERY

For Reading and Meditation: Ecclesiastes 8:9–15

"... joy will accompany him in his work all the days of [his] life ..." (v. 15)

This section begins with a warning for those who are in positions of authority. *Those who lord it over others in an unfair way will hurt themselves more than they hurt others.* It might feel good to ride roughshod over people's thoughts and feelings, but in the end the one who acts in this way is demeaned as a person. He becomes less of a human being – a consequence every leader ought to work strenuously to avoid.

From here Solomon focuses on several mysteries, things we are all aware of, but for which we have no really clear answers. The first is this – wicked people being praised at their funeral (v. 10). Ever witnessed such a situation? It bothered Solomon so much he called it "meaningless". A second thing that mystified Solomon was why a sentence for a crime is not quickly carried out (v. 11). If Solomon was living in our day when rapists and psychopaths on remand are let out to re-enact their crimes, he would not simply say it is meaningless – he would go berserk.

A third thing that mystified the wise king is something he has mentioned once before – the mystery of how Providence seems to treat the good as though they were wicked and the wicked as though they were good. We discussed this issue earlier, but there is no clear or adequate explanation. It still remains a mystery even when you have said all you have to say. Solomon's way of dealing with mystery is quite simple: eat, drink, and put your trust in God (v. 15). In other words, continue the routines of life and keep going even though the mysteries remain unsolved. With God we can cope with anything that comes, even though we can't explain it.

With God we can cope with any- thing that comes, even though we can't explain it.

Father, I see that if I can take this fact on board then I have one of the greatest keys to life. Help me to still serve You and love You even in the absence of explanation. This I ask in Jesus' Name. Amen.

IT'S BETTER TO TRUST

For Reading and Meditation: Ecclesiastes 8:16–17

"Even if a wise man claims he knows, he cannot really comprehend [what goes on under the sun]." (v. 17)

The sooner we come to terms with the fact that there are things which happen in life for which there is no adequate explanation, the better we shall be. I have seen people almost drive themselves insane by insisting that God was honour-bound to give them a clear answer or explanation for some dark or difficult situation into which they were plunged.

Now it is not wrong to desire answers from God, but as I have said before, when those desires escalate into a demand – we head for trouble. Some things that happen here on earth defy explanation. We must accept that and live with it. Life "under the sun" will always be a puzzle or, as Winston Churchill put it when trying to negotiate with Communist Russia: "a riddle wrapped in a mystery inside an enigma". Once we stop trying to find the missing pieces to the puzzles of life and get on with the task of living, the more effectively (forgive the mixed metaphors) will we be able to channel our energies in the right direction. Just remember that the missing pieces of every puzzle in your life are in the hands of the One who put this universe together in the first place.

Life: "a riddle wrapped in a mystery inside an enigma".

Derek Tidball tells the story of a small boy who was bullied by some other boys because they said his father was a Frankenstein who put people to sleep, cut them open, took out parts and put in others. The boy's father, of course, was a surgeon. The little boy, however, was untroubled because he knew and trusted his father and was aware that even though he could not understand why his father did the things he did, he would not be involved in anything that was evil or bad. It is the same with God.

O Father, help me drop my anchor into the depths of this reassuring and encouraging revelation – there is a good reason for everything You do. May I trust You even when I cannot trace You. In Jesus' Name I ask it. Amen.

TURNING THE CORNER

For Reading and Meditation: Ecclesiastes 9:1–6

*"For the living know that they will die,
but the dead know nothing ..." (v. 5)*

I n this chapter Solomon continues to break with cynicism and focuses our gaze more clearly on the issues that are "above the sun". Four simple facts are laid out in this passage – facts that every believer should know and understand.

The first is this – *everything is in God's hands* (v. 1). When I think of myself as being in "God's hands" I feel tremendously reassured. Nothing can get out of control. Matters may seem out of control to me, but not to Him. It is true, as Solomon says, that "no man knows whether love or hate awaits him" (v. 1). But when we have God, then nothing will ever confront us that we (He and we) can't handle together. Look now at the second fact – *the certainty of death* (vv. 2–3). Death is a common destiny for all; it is a debt everyone must pay. But how blessed are those whose goals reach beyond death, and who have a settled and assured eternal future with God. Anyone who lives only for time is a fool. I hope, by the way, you have settled the question in your own heart about where you are going to spend eternity.

The third fact is this – *madness resides in the human spirit* (v. 3). Don't expect too much of humanity and you won't be disappointed. One of the best descriptions of sin I know is insanity. It is sheer insanity to think we can run our lives successfully without recourse to God. Yet most of humanity try to do it every day. Utter madness! And now the last fact – *where there's life there's hope* (vv. 4–6). "Better a live dog than a dead lion," says Solomon (v. 4). Why? Because the king of the jungle when dead has no hope. As long as there's life there's a chance dreams can come true, that plans can be realised, but, above all, that one's eternal destiny can be settled.

Matters may seem out of control to me, but not to Him.

Father, I see that along with life comes the presence of hope. Help me now, while I am alive, to know for certain that I will spend eternity with You. I yield myself to You today. In Jesus' Name. Amen.

"GO ... WITH GLADNESS"

For Reading and Meditation: Ecclesiastes 9:7–10

"Always be clothed in white, and always anoint your head with oil." (v. 8)

We ended yesterday with the thought that where there's life there's hope. The section before us today picks up on that thought and continues it.

"Go, eat your food with gladness," Solomon says, "and drink your wine with a joyful heart" (v. 7). Hedonists reading these words might think: "Just what I want ... freedom to go out and indulge myself." But hold on, read the next line: "Always be clothed in white, and always anoint your head with oil" (v. 8). That isn't to be taken literally, of course. It is a symbolic statement meaning – keep yourself clean. Solomon is not giving us permission to gorge ourselves, but to focus on one day at a time and enjoy every day as it comes. A paraphrase of what he is saying here which might be helpful is this: "The arguments for the meaninglessness of life are powerful – injustice, suffering, sudden death, criminals getting away with murder while the good die in penury and shame. My mind tells me to give up the search for meaning because there isn't any. But as I reflect on God, I find my heart beating again with the hope that I shall spend eternity with Him. Because of that I can go on, eating my food with gladness and drinking my wine with a joyful heart."

Solomon's counsel continues: husbands, enjoy your wives (v. 9). Enjoy, not put up with. You have a wife? Love her. Live it up and have fun in your marriage. Don't wait until you retire to enjoy life. Then Solomon adds: "Whatever your hand finds to do, do it with all your might" (v. 10). The only things some people throw themselves into is their beds at night – weary, and utterly spent. They don't enjoy life; simply endure it. You enjoy God, enjoy living too.

Focus on one day at a time and enjoy every day as it comes.

Gracious loving heavenly Father, save me from thinking that I must wait until I die before I live. I will live more fully then, but help me to throw myself fully into life in the here and now also. In Jesus' Name I ask it. Amen.

For Reading and Meditation: Ecclesiastes 9:11–12

"... time and chance happen to them all." (v. 11)

Before moving on, an explanation is necessary for Solomon's reference to death which we read about in the verses we dealt with yesterday: "In the grave, where you are going, there is neither working nor planning nor knowledge nor wisdom" (v. 10). Death, to the Old Testament saints, was a mystery. They believed in life after death, but they were not sure of the quality of that life. Thus death is often spoken of in negative terms. Only since Christ came and defeated death have we been able to see it in its true perspective. This has to be kept in mind when reading the phrase I have referred to.

In the previous verses of this chapter Solomon gave us one side of the coin; in today's section he gives us the other side. He is concerned that his instruction to enjoy ourselves is not taken too far, and we get caught up, as so many do, in what is often described as "the rat race". "The race is not to the swift," he says, "or the battle to the strong ..." (v. 11). The philosophy that drives most people nowadays is this: if you want to get on, run faster than anyone else. That philosophy is for empty-headed rats, not people. People who love God and want to honour Him will resist that pressure. You can build a good business and be competitive without spending your life in the fast lane.

True success is walking with God. Keep in mind the fact that everything is in God's hands, Solomon once again reminds us. Things happen when you least expect them. Stock markets go down, somebody withholds a payment and a business collapses. Nothing is certain in this world. God alone knows the end from the beginning – hence the need to put your entire trust in Him.

True success is walking with God.

Father, I see through new eyes the truth that the strong are not always the strongest, the clever are not always the cleverest. I am challenged to discover a new place of trust in my life. My trust, blessed Father, is in You. All in You. Amen.

A TALE OF ONE CITY

For Reading and Meditation: Ecclesiastes 9:13–18

"The quiet words of the wise are more to be heeded than the shouts of a ruler of fools." (v. 17)

Solomon addresses the issue we were discussing yesterday – avoiding getting caught in the rat race – by putting it in the form of a story. Imagine, he says, a small city with only a few people in it. Suddenly an invading army surrounds the city and puts it under siege. Inside the city is a wise but poor man who comes up with an idea that saves the city. We are not told what the idea was, but we are told that when the city was saved, the poor man was forgotten. The punch line is this: "Wisdom is better than strength" (v. 16). Strength is more impressive than wisdom, but in the long run wisdom is the more effective. One writer says of this parable: "It is not a moral tale to show what people should do, but a cautionary tale to show what they are like." People easily forget or overlook the importance of wisdom, and Solomon is reminding us that we should take this into account so that we are not surprised when it happens. The way of the world is this – be strong, be smart, be clever, be competitive, get one over the other person before they get one over on you. But when trouble strikes and people are under threat, they are ready to listen to wise words that get them out of trouble. Then, when the crisis is over, they forget what they heard and go back to being strong again.

Enemy forces surround us. We are under threat. Marriages are crumbling, and the moral ropes that once held us so fast and firm are now frayed or burning. We have a book called the Bible which contains the wisdom the world needs. We must draw more attention to it. People may listen, or they may not, but that is not our responsibility. We must speak so that God can work.

People easily forget or overlook the importance of wisdom.

Father, I realise that if wisdom is to come through me then it must first reside in me. Make me a man or woman of the Book. May my mind be soaked in the wisdom of Scripture so that when I speak my words become Your words. In Christ's Name I ask it. Amen.

For Reading and Meditation: Ecclesiastes 11:1–4

"Give portions to seven,
yes to eight ..." (v. 2)

Solomon's cynicism almost completely dissolves as we step into these last chapters. If you are like me, you are probably saying to yourself: "And not before time!" He begins this chapter with a saying that is oft repeated and well known: "Cast your bread upon the waters, for after many days you will find it again" (v. 1). What Solomon is conveying in these words is this: "Be generous, share yourself with others." I like Charles Swindoll's paraphrase of this verse, which reads thus: "Don't put the bread in the deep freeze – it'll dry out. Release it." The main thought underlying this statement is not simply to give, but to give boldly, enthusiastically, and energetically.

We are powerless to change certain things, like the weather for instance. When clouds are full of rain they drench the earth, says Solomon. And where the stick falls it lies.

There is simply no point in focusing on the things that are unchangeable and allowing our thoughts to become preoccupied with these issues. Far better to get on with living and work at changing the things that can be changed. A sign on a rough unmade road somewhere in northern Canada reads: "Choose your rut carefully. You'll be in it for the next 200 miles." Solomon's advice is that we should do everything in our power to stay out of ruts.

Have you settled for a drab, predictable life when you could be using your God-given creativity to explore new things and new horizons? Don't just drift through life – pursue it. Turn your gaze to new activities and new ideas. Don't stop being creative. Don't get into a rut. Shame on you that you stand around and just watch the wind. Don't drift like a lazy cloud. Pursue something new and beautiful for God.

"Be generous, share yourself with others."

O God, forgive me that I spend so much time worrying about such things as whether it's going to rain or shine, instead of pursuing new things and new purposes. I'm through with all that, dear Lord. I'm choosing life. In Jesus' Name. Amen.

"DO NOT DISTURB!"

For Reading and Meditation: Ecclesiastes 11:5–6

"… you cannot understand the work of God,
the Maker of all things." (v. 5)

There are some things in life that, try as we might, we will never fully understand. I'm not sure I understand how a black cow eats green grass and gives white milk, but it doesn't stop me enjoying a glass of it now and again!

This is Solomon's point in the verses before us today. We don't know which course the wind will take, or how bones are formed in a tiny foetus, but it happens anyway. And why? Because God is at work in everything, and the best thing we can do is trust Him. Modern-day science has naturally cleared up many things that were mysteries to the men and women who lived thousands of years ago, but we are still faced with a good deal of unexplained phenomena nevertheless. I am not against scientific research providing it stays within ethical guidelines. However, whether mysteries can be explained or not – we must carry on living.

"Sow in the morning and don't be idle in the evening" is Solomon's next word. He is not saying, of course, that we ought to work all through the day, or that it is wrong to have a time of leisure and relaxation; rather, he is pointing out the benefits of having other interests besides work. There is something wrong in the lives of those who, having finished their day's work, hang a sign on the door of their lives that says: "Do Not Disturb." If, after your day's work, you are too tired to focus on something else then perhaps you ought to re-evaluate your whole lifestyle. It's easy for me to tell you that because I've just done it myself. And I feel much better for it. Solomon's advice came to me at a crucial moment in my life, and unless I'm mistaken, today is going to be crucial and challenging for some of you too.

God is at work in everything, and the best thing we can do is trust Him.

O God, help me today to take a prayerful and careful look at my lifestyle. Am I really living – or just going through one dreary day after another? Teach me how to pursue life, not have it pursuing me. In Jesus' Name. Amen.

IT'S GREAT TO BE ALIVE!

For Reading and Meditation: Ecclesiastes 11:7–10

*"However many years a man may live,
let him enjoy them all." (v. 8)*

D o you need permission to enjoy life? Then Solomon gives it to you in these verses. The Moffatt translation of verse 7 reads: "Sweet is the light of life, and pleasant is it for the eyes to see the sun." Whilst Solomon is clearly talking about natural light, we must see also that these words are symbolic. God is often spoken of in terms of light and warmth. The light of God's love is ever present.

The joy of living, he goes on to say, ought to permeate every period of our lives, right up to old age. "If a man live many years, let him have joy throughout them all" (v. 7, Moffatt). This is not to ignore the fact, of course, that many have had some pretty rough experiences in life – evils such as sexual and physical abuse, rejection, abandonment, and so on – but with good Christian counselling these experiences can be overcome. Indeed, Solomon recommends remembering the days of darkness, for when you experience the light and love of God you can look back at painful events without the loss of your soul. You are pained by the memories of them, but not overwhelmed. In fact, the dark days throw into even greater relief the brightness of the joy that comes from God.

Solomon's final comments in this chapter are aimed at the young. Enjoy your days one by one, he is saying, because before you know it, you will be an adult. The words that come next have sent some Christians into apoplexy: "Follow the ways of your heart and whatever your eyes see ..." (v. 9). This is what Solomon is really saying: "Relax and have a super time when you are young. There will many impulses and many things that appeal to your eyes. Follow them, but keep in mind there will be a day of accountability. So don't let your impulses go wild, and don't let the things that appeal to your eyes lead you into illegitimate areas of living."

Dark days throw into even greater relief the brightness of the joy that comes from God.

Thank You, my Father, for reminding me that there is no freedom without limitations. Help me see the wisdom that lies behind Your restrictions, and enable me to trust You and follow You all the days of my life. In Christ's Name I ask it. Amen.

For Reading and Meditation: Ecclesiastes 12:1

*"Remember your Creator in the days of your youth,
before the days of trouble come ..." (v. 1)*

At long last we are introduced in the most clear terms to
the only One who can give life meaning – God. I
suspect Solomon has been wanting to say this from the very
beginning, but like a good preacher, he keeps his best point
to the last.

There's another reason, however, why God has not been
brought clearly into the picture until now – some people
need to feel and experience the utter futility of trying to
quench the deep thirsts of their souls in any other way but
in God. An Hassadic story tells of a man who went for a
walk in a forest and got lost. He wandered around for hours
attempting to find his way back home, trying one path and
then another. Suddenly he came across another traveller
who was also lost, and together they sat down to discuss
what they could do. "I know" said one, "let's tell each other
what paths we have tried and then it will be that much
easier to find our way out." They did, and within a few
hours both emerged safely from the forest. This is how
many people find God – they try one meaningless path after
another until, in the end, they find the Way.

The point Solomon wants to press home in the verse
before us today is that the best time to know God is when
one is young. It is perilously possible that if the opportunity
to open one's heart is not taken in youth, then procras-
tination can build strong resistance in the soul that makes it
difficult (though not impossible) to respond in later life. I
gave my life to God when I was in my mid teens. Now,
close on five decades later, I thrill to the thought that not
only have I known Him, but I have had the privilege of
serving Him also. Believe me, there can be no greater joy.

*The best
time to
know God
is when
one is
young.*

O Father, I can testify to that too – there is no greater joy than
knowing You and serving You. And as long as I am on this
earth, may the wonder of both these privileges increase and
abound. In Jesus' Name I pray. Amen.

THE PLUS OF THE SPIRIT

For Reading and Meditation: Ecclesiastes 12:2–4

"... those looking through the windows
grow dim ..." (v. 3)

We are now drawn into a picture of very old age that might be a little too vivid for our liking. Solomon's purpose is to point out the advantages of serving God while young, and to convince us of his counsel to remember our Creator in the days of our youth. We can serve God in old age (as we have seen), but the reality is that very old age slows us down somewhat and we can't give as much energy to the work of God as once we did.

Verse 2 talks about mental aging. The sun and the light, which are symbols here of clarity and sharpness, recede, and the darkness begins to descend on the mind. Verse 3 focuses on physical deterioration when "the keepers of the house tremble". It is thought that the term "keepers of the house" refers to our limbs which in very old age begin to tremble and become weak. We are left, also, with few teeth (at least of our own), and this is what is thought to lie behind the expression "when the grinders cease because they are few". Verse 3 speaks of the eyes growing dim, and verse 4 speaks of being shut in and of enforced inactivity: "the doors to the streets are closed and the sound of grinding fades." The latter part of the verse reminds us that even sleep becomes difficult for those who are old – the elderly are usually awake with what we call the dawn chorus. But unfortunately some are not even able to hear the singing of the birds because their hearing is no longer acute. They suffer a double denial – sleeplessness and deafness. Young people find it difficult to believe that is the way they will be one day (if, of course, they live long enough), but that is the reality. Therefore, young people, give God your best – while you can.

Give God your best – while you can.

Father, I know I have to face reality, but I know too that the touch of Your Spirit can be upon me when I grow old. Sustain me through all the years of my life so that I might know the plus of Your Spirit as well as the plus of the years. Amen.

For Reading and Meditation: Ecclesiastes 12:5–8

"Remember him – before the silver cord is severed ..." (v. 6)

Can you handle another day focusing on the charac-teristics of old age? Well, remember the ability to face reality is one of the most clear evidences of mental health! You don't have to dwell on the facts as they relate to old age, but you do have to face them. That is all Solomon is saying.

Four more characteristics are given in verse 5. First, fear – fear of heights and being out in busy streets. Second, the appearance of grey hair. Clearly, the phrase "the almond tree blossoms" is a reference to the head of silver hair. Third, the difficulty of walking – "the grasshopper drags himself along." One has a picture here of walking frames or walking sticks. As you know, it takes old people a little longer to get where they want to go! Fourth, the waning of the sex drive. I don't know if being last on the list means the sex drive is the last thing to go. Some studies show that it is. In verse 6 Solomon returns to the point he made in the opening verse of the chapter – remember Him. Remember God, he reminds us, before "the silver cord is severed or the golden bowl is broken". These graphic word pictures (and the ones that follow) all point to death.

Now to stop just there would be gloomy indeed, but Solomon gives us something to lift our hearts: "the spirit returns to God who gave it" (v. 7). Death, to those who love God, is not the end, but the beginning; the majestic commencement of what life is all about – union with God. To those who do not know God, however, death is a transition from emptiness to even greater emptiness (v. 8). Those who know how to live know also how to die.

Death, to those who love God, is not the end, but the beginning.

O God, I am so thankful for the victory that Christ wrought for me over the grave. He "brought life and immortality to light through the gospel". Help me to live in that victory from one day to another. In Jesus' Name I ask it. Amen.

THE MARKS OF A PREACHER

For Reading and Meditation: Ecclesiastes 12:9–10

"The Teacher searched to find just the right words ..." (v. 10)

In these last few verses Solomon moves into a brief autobiographical section. These are a wise man's studied reflections and conclusions. The Preacher opens up his heart and tells us what a preacher should be like. There are five characteristics or marks.

First and foremost a preacher should be wise. He gets this wisdom not from his years, but from his communication with God. Second, he should be able to impart knowledge to others – help them understand the principles on which a godly life is built. Third, he must ponder things, reflect on them, and search them out; wrestle with them as a dog wrestles with a bone. Fourth, he must then set those things in a logical order and sequence. In doing this he must pay particular attention to the use of proverbs, says Solomon – something we seem to miss out on in this day and generation. One Christian writer says: "Ours may be the first generation in civilised times that has not raised its young on proverbs." A sad comment, don't you think?

Fifth, a preacher should be able to search out and use the right words. A preacher depends on the Holy Spirit, of course, but he needs words to make his meaning clear. And not just words, but the right words. "The difference between the right word and the almost right word," said Mark Twain, "is the difference between a lightning flash and a firefly." The words of a good preacher are like windows through which the light of truth shines. Undoubtedly, Solomon exemplified all these five characteristics. Would that there were more like him in the community of God's people today.

"The difference between the right word and the almost right word is the difference between a lightning flash and a firefly."

My Father and my God, give us more preachers, we pray, who know You and who know their craft. Work by Your Spirit in the hearts of those You have called to preach, so that the next generation might not be failed. In Jesus' Name we ask it. Amen.

IMPROVING OUR ADJECTIVES

For Reading and Meditation: Ecclesiastes 12:11

"The words of the wise are like goads, their collected sayings, like firmly embedded nails ..." (v. 11)

Living as he did in an agricultural community, it is easy to see why Solomon likens words to goads. A goad is a long stick with an iron point that is jabbed against the hindquarters of an animal to make it increase its speed. Words motivate and urge us to action.

J. B. Phillips used a different picture to illustrate the same point: "If words are to enter men's hearts and bear fruit, they must be the right words, shaped cunningly to pass men's defences and explode silently and effectually within their minds." Isn't this how Solomon used words? His graphic word pictures have brought me up sharply on more than one occasion, I can tell you.

Words and wise sayings are also like firmly embedded nails, says Solomon. Even that very phrase catches hold of the imagination. It recalls for me a vivid phrase I once heard Sir Winston Churchill use of one of his Generals. "He reminds me," he said, "of an iron peg hammered into the frozen ground – firm, solid, immovable." And here's a personal confession – one of the reasons why I use so much alliteration (words with the same initial sound) is to help you remember them. This for example: "Eat enough to keep you fit and not enough to make you fat." I know people remember these statements because they sometimes quote them back to me. We must use the best and the most precise words we can when talking about Christ, remembering all the time, as C. S. Lewis said, that we are just adjectives striving to point others to the Noun. "And for people to believe that Noun", he added, "we must improve our adjectives."

"If words are to enter men's hearts and bear fruit, they must be the right words."

O Father, help me understand that it is not increasing my vocabulary that You are after, but doing the best with what I already have. You deserve nothing but the best. May I therefore be the best I can be. In Jesus' Name. Amen.

A PERSON OF THE BOOK

For Reading and Meditation: Ecclesiastes 12:12

"Be warned, my son, of anything in addition to them." (v. 12)

Solomon seems to have held off counselling his son until now, and what he said to him will go down well with those of you who are students and are involved in much study.

First, he counsels his son not to put too much trust in words or books that go beyond the Scriptures. I think Moffatt best captures the thought of Solomon in his translation of this verse, which reads thus: "My son, avoid anything beyond the scriptures of wisdom; there is no end to the buying of books, and to study books closely is weariness to the flesh." The trouble with books is that you have to read a lot to get a little. That is not the same, however, with the Scriptures. "All Scripture," said Paul to Timothy, "is inspired by God and is profitable ..." (2 Tim. 3:16, RSV). If we were to spend as much time in the Bible as we do in books about the Bible, we might be better off spiritually. Solomon is not saying that we ought to read nothing but the Scriptures; rather that we ought to make the study of the Scriptures our top priority.

In my time I have studied many subjects – psychology, sociology, communication, and so on. I frankly confess that I found many of these subjects tiresome. The same cannot be said of Scripture, however. When I open the Book of books, the Bible, I come to it with an enthusiasm, an eagerness and an expectancy that is not there with any other book. I hope you share that same experience too. Reading a daily Bible aid such as *Every Day with Jesus* may help you with your daily devotions (I pray that it does), but don't let it take the place of Scripture in your life. Believe me, I would be heartbroken if I thought it did.

We ought to make the study of the Scriptures our top priority.

O God my Father, whilst I am thankful for all the books that help me learn of You and know about You, help me never to put these ahead of Your Word, the Bible, but always behind it. Make me a person of the Book. Amen.

THE END OF THE SEARCH

For Reading and Meditation: Ecclesiastes 12:13–14

"For God will bring every deed into judgment ... whether it is good or evil." (v. 14)

This is our final day together when our exploration of Ecclesiastes comes to an end. We have travelled with Solomon over many roads, and have listened to a wide variety of reflections, some of which we may have thought were tedious, repetitive, and tendentious. The world does not have the resources to meet the needs of the soul, he has been saying, and any attempt to try to find meaning in life apart from God is utterly futile. *Meaning comes only when we attach ourselves to God.*

It all boils down to this, is his penultimate statement – "Fear God and keep his commandments" (v. 13). To "fear God" means we must reverence Him and put Him first. To "keep his commandments" means we obey Him whether we feel like it or not. Some see Solomon's concluding words as an anti-climax. No graphic word picture, no impressive or catchy sayings. But then this is the art of evangelism. Winning souls does not mean forcing the gospel down people's throats, but quietly going with them down one road after another and showing them that this is not where life is found, then quietly bringing them back without fuss or fanfare to the inescapable conclusion that the one true reality is God.

Solomon's last statement is simple yet quite staggering: "God will bring every deed into judgment ... whether it is good or evil." Why such a solemn note to end? Because we can't live irresponsibly and get away with it. We can't buck the universe. God always has the last word. How do we sum up the message of Ecclesiastes? Like this: fear God and serve Him because one day you are going to stand before Him. I'm ready. Are you?

Fear God and serve Him because one day you are going to stand before Him.

My Father and my God, if I am not ready then let Your Spirit be in my heart, and help me make the decision to turn my life over to You today. I do so now in humble repentance and simple trust. Take me, cleanse me, and make me Your child. In Jesus' Name! Amen.